First published in Great Britain in 1996 by

BROCKHAMPTON PRESS,

20 Bloomsbury Street,

London WC1B 3QA.

a member of the Hodder Headline Group,

This series of little gift books was made by Frances Banfield, Andrea P.A. Belloli, Polly Boyd, Kate Brown, Stefano Carantini, Laurel Clark, Penny Clarke, Clive Collins, Jack Cooper, Melanie Cumming, Nick Diggory, John Dunne, Deborah Gill, David Goodman, Paul Gregory, Douglas Hall, Lucinda Hawksley, Maureen Hill, Dennis Hovell, Dicky Howett, Nick Hutchison, Douglas Ingram, Helen Johnson, C.M. Lee, Simon London, Irene Lyford, John Maxwell, Patrick McCreeth, Morse Modaberi, Tara Neill, Sonya Newland, Anne Newman, Grant Oliver, Ian Powling, Terry Price, Michelle Rogers, Mike Seabrook, Nigel Soper, Karen Sullivan and Nick Wells.

Compilation and selection copyright © 1996 Brockhampton Press.

ISBN 1 86019 4273

A copy of the CIP data is available from the British Library upon request.

Produced for Brockhampton Press by Flame Tree Publishing, a part of The Foundry Creative Media Company Limited, The Long House, Antrobus Road, Chiswick W4 5HY.

Printed and bound in Italy by L.E.G.O. Spa.

THE LITTLE BOOK
OF
Horses
& Ponies

Selected by Karen Sullivan

BROCKHAMPTON PRESS

I find that a heavy cold clears up if the sufferer
kisses a mule's muzzle.

Pliny the Elder, *Natural History*

I've often said there's nothing better for the inside of
a man than the outside of a horse.

Ronald Reagan

The horse, the horse! The symbol of surging potency
and power of movement, of action, in man.

D. H. Lawrence

In 1891, a horse called Linus
lived in the American state of Oregon,
the possessor of a tail nine feet long,
a mane seven feet and ten inches long,
and a forelock five and a half feet long.

Who has a good horse in his stable can go afoot.

Proverb

Animals are such agreeable friends —
they ask no questions, they pass no criticisms.

George Eliot, *Scenes of Clerical Life*

The air of heaven is that which blows
between a horse's ears.

Arab proverb

They say Princes learn no art truly, but the art of
horsemanship. The reason is, the brave beast is no
flatterer. He will throw a prince as soon as his groom.

Ben Jonson

It takes a good deal of physical courage to ride a horse.
This, however, I have. I get it at about forty cents a
flask, and take it as required.

Stephen Leacock

Hast thou given the horse strength?
Hast thou clothed his neck with thunder?
Canst thou make him afraid as a grasshopper?
The glory of his nostrils is terrible. He paweth in the
valley, and rejoiceth in his strength: he goeth on to
meet the armed men. He saith among the trumpets,
Ha, ha;
and he smelleth the battle afar off,
the thunder of the captains, and the shouting.

Job, XXXIX:19–25

Though I am an old horse, and have seen and heard a
great deal, I never yet could make out why men are so
fond of this sport; they often hurt themselves,
often spoil good horses, and tear up the fields,

and all for a hare, or a fox, or a stag, that they could
get more easily some other way;
but we are only horses, and don't know.

Anna Sewell, *Black Beauty*

Have a horse of thine own
and thou mayst borrow another's.

Welsh proverb

My beautiful, my beautiful!
That standest meekly by,
With thy proudly-arched and glossy neck,
and dark and fiery eye!

Caroline Sheridan Norton

Men are not hanged for stealing horses,
but that horses may not be stolen.

Lord George Savile Halifax

The Roman emperor Caligula loved his horse Incitatus
so much that he invited him to supper, giving him wine
to drink, and later made him a priest and a consul.

There may have been many faster horses, no doubt
many handsomer, but for bottom and endurance
I never saw his fellow.

The Duke of Wellington on his horse Copenhagen

The man who does not love a horse
cannot love a woman.

Spanish proverb

A fly, Sir, may sting a stately horse and
make him wince; but one is but an insect,
and the other is a horse still.

Samuel Johnson

We are told that in the thirteenth century, a horse was
exhibited by the joculators, which danced upon a rope.

Joseph Strutt, *Sports and Pastimes of the People of England*

Such panting and blowing! Such spreading
and contracting of the red equine nostrils,
and glaring of the wild equine eye!

Mark Twain, *Roughing It*

He was an awkward, ignorant rustic of the lowest class,
of the name of Sullivan, but better known as the
Whisperer. His occupation was horse-breaking, and his
nickname he acquired from the notion of his being able
to communicate to the animal what he wished by
means of a whisper.

William Youatt, *The Horse*

If two men ride a horse, one must ride behind.

Proverb

'Bring forth the horse!' – the horse was brought;
In truth, he was a noble steed,
A Tartar of the Ukraine breed,
Who looked as though the speed of thought
Were in his limbs.

Lord Byron, 'Mazeppa'

And now, as proud as a King of Spain,
He moved in his box with a restless tread,
His eyes like sparks in his lovely head.

John Masefield, 'Right Royal'

One may ride a free horse to death.

Scottish proverb

It is the prince of palfreys;
his neigh is like the bidding of a monarch
and his countenance enforces homage.

William Shakespeare, *Henry V*

When I bestride him, I soar, I am a hawk: he trots the
air; the earth sings when he touches it; the basest horn
of his hoof is more musical than the pipe of Hermes.

William Shakespeare, *Henry V*

Sleipnir was Odin's eight-footed grey horse, which
could traverse both land and sea.
The horse represents the wind, which blows from the
eight principal points of the compass.

John Gilpin at his horse's side
Seiz'd fast the flowing mane,
And up he got, in haste to ride,
But soon came down again.

William Cowper, 'The Diverting History of John Gilpin'

The stable wears out a horse more than the road.

French proverb

❧ 20 ❧

Where would she find him? There were so many places he might be: the stables, the pine-wood, the kitchen garden, the cricket-field, the Play House – where should she look first? She decided to try the stables, for even if they were not there, Tom might know where his cousins were. She turned to the left, and going up the hill to the stable yard, found Tom in a loose-box, gravely pulling hairs out of the tail of Chuck, the big brown hunter. Her grandfather kept three horses, two to ride and one to drive in the dog-cart, and there were three hairy ponies for the children running loose in the Park. 'If yew're looking for Master Denys,' said Tom, accompanying each word with a tweak at the tail of the wincing Chuck, ''e come up here 'bout half an hour ago...'

Monica Dickens, *Mariana*

He can't keep still, the ears prick up,
the limbs quiver, He drinks the air,
he jets it in hot steam out of his nostrils.

Virgil, 'Georgics'

One cannot shoe a running horse.

Dutch proverb

If he hears armour clang in the distance,
According to Norse legend, the horse of Night is
Hrimfaxi, 'Frost-mane', from whose bit fall the rime-
drops which nightly bedew the earth.

Boot, saddle, to horse, and away!

Robert Browning, *Cavalier Tunes*

In Christian art, the horse is held
to represent courage and generosity.

I sit astride life like a bad rider on a horse.
I only owe it to the horse's good nature that I am not
thrown off at this very moment.

Ludwig Wittgenstein

Five and twenty ponies
Trotting through the dark –
Brandy for the Parson,
Baccy for the Clerk;
Laces for a lady, letters for a spy,
Watch the wall, my darling,
while the Gentlemen go by!

Rudyard Kipling, 'A Smuggler's Song'

A man may lead a horse to water,
but he cannot make him drink.

English proverb

Lord Ronald flung himself upon his horse and rode
madly off in all directions.

Stephen Leacock, *Nonsense Novels*

I know two things about the horse,
And one of them is rather coarse.

Anonymous, *The Weekend Book*

All lay load on the willing horse.

English proverb

Ride a cock-horse to Banbury Cross,
To see a fine lady upon a white horse,
Rings on her fingers and bells on her toes,
She shall have music wherever she goes.

Nursery rhyme

The old horse may die waiting for the new grass.

Chinese proverb

A horse! A horse! My kingdom for a horse!

William Shakespeare, *King Richard III*

Good horses can't be of a bad colour.

Gypsy proverb

He doth nothing but talk of his horse.

William Shakespeare, *The Merchant of Venice*

To God I speak Spanish, to women Italian,
to men French, and to my horse, German.

King Charles V

Only a man harrowing clods
In a slow silent walk
With an old horse that stumbles and nods
Half asleep as they stalk.

Thomas Hardy, 'Friends Beyond'

One man may better steal a horse
than another look on.

English proverb

Come fill up my cup, come fill up my can,
Come saddle your horses, and call up your men;
Come open the West Port, and let me gang free,
And it's room for the bonnets of Bonny Dundee!

Walter Scott, 'Bonny Dundee'

Some put their trust in chariots, and some in horses:
but we will remember the name of the Lord our God.

Book of Common Prayer

I race
and my mane catches the wind.
I race,
falling over my own feet in my joy.

Carmen Bernos de Gasztold, 'The Prayer of the Foal'

A horse is dangerous at both ends
and unsafe in the middle.

Ian Fleming

The steed bit his master.
How came this to pass?
He heard the good pastor
Cry, 'All flesh is grass.'

Anonymous

There are two important rules for riding.
The first is to mount the horse.
The second is to stay mounted.

Anonymous

For the want of a nail, the shoe was lost,
For the want of a shoe, the horse was lost,
For want of a horse, the rider was lost,
For want of a rider, the battle was lost,
For the want of a battle, the kingdom was lost,
And all for the want of a horseshoe nail.

Benjamin Franklin

Lord Hippo suffered fearful loss
By putting money on a horse
Which he believed, if it were pressed,
Would run far faster than the rest.

Hilaire Belloc, 'Cautionary Verse'

My purpose is, indeed, a horse of that colour.

William Shakespeare, *Twelfth Night*

If wishes were horses,
Beggars would ride.

Proverb

Baby's
First Ride.

The wild forest, the clothed holts with green,
With reins avaled, and swift breathed horse,
With cry of hounds and merry blasts between,
Where we did chase the fearful hart a force.

Henry Howard, Earl of Surrey

Forgiveness, horse! why do I rail on thee,
Since thou, created to be awed by man,
Wast born to bear?

William Shakespeare, *Richard II*

Round-hoofed, short jointed, fetlocks shag and long,
Broad breast, full eye, small head, and nostrils wide,
High crest, short ears, straight legs and passing strong,
Thin mane, thick tail, broad buttock, tender hide:
Look, what a horse should have he did not lack,
Save a proud rider on so proud a back.

William Shakespeare, 'Venus and Adonis'

And when the horse was loose, off to the fen
Through thick and thin, and whinneying 'Weehee!'
He raced to join the wild mares running free.

Geoffrey Chaucer, *The Reeve's Tale*

War horses are useless for victory;
their great strength cannot save.

Psalms

In 1888 a horse in Manchester was fitted with
spectacles to correct short sight. At first the horse was a
little surprised, but rapidly showed signs of the keenest
pleasure, and took to standing all morning looking over
the half-door of his stable with his spectacles on, gazing
around him with an air of sedate enjoyment.

I looked, and there was a pale-coloured horse.
Its rider was named death.

Revelation

He grew into his seat,
And to such wondrous doing brought his horse,
As he had been incorps'd and demi-natur'd
With the brave beast.

William Shakespeare, *Hamlet*

His angry steede did chide his foming bitt,
As much disdayning to the curbe to yield.

Edmund Spenser, 'The Fairie Queene'

We tolerate shapes in human beings that would
horrify us if we saw them in a horse.

W. R. Inge

Hard is to teach an old horse to amble trew.

Edmund Spenser, 'The Fairie Queene'

I am that merry wanderer of the night.
I jest to Oberon, and make him smile
When I a fat and bean-fed horse beguile,
Neighing in likeness of a filly foal.

William Shakespeare, *A Midsummer Night's Dream*

Look when a painter would surpass the life,
In limning out a well proportioned steed,
His art with nature's workmanship at strife,
As if the dead the living should exceed;
So did this horse excel a common one,
In shape, in courage, colour, pace and bone.

William Shakespeare, 'Venus and Adonis'

Fix this sentence:
He put the horse before the cart.

Stephen Price

Horsepower was a wonderful thing,
when only horses had it.

Anonymous

Men are generally more careful of the breed of their
horses and dogs than of their children.

William Penn, *Reflexions and Maxims*

England is a paradise for women, and hell for horses:
Italy a paradise for horses, hell for women,
as the proverb goes.

Robert Burton, *Anatomy of Melancholy*

On the right were the pony lines, where incredibly
polished ponies, tied to iron rails in the shade of a row
of horse chestnuts, were stamping, nudging,
flattening ears at each other and aiming
kicks at any fly eating their bellies.
God, they were beautiful, thought Perdita longingly,
and curiously naked and vulnerable with their
hogged manes and bound-up tails.

Jilly Cooper, *Polo*

Now see him mounted once again
Upon his nimble steed,
Full slowly pacing o'er the stones
With caution and good heed.

William Cowper, 'The Diverting History of John Gilpin'

Go anywhere in England where there are natural,
wholesome, contented and really nice English people,
and what do you always find? That the stables are the
real centre of the household.

George Bernard Shaw, *Heartbreak House*

And I saw my stout Roland at last,
With resolute shoulders, each butting away
The haze, as some bluff river headland its spray
And his low head and crest,
just one sharp ear bent back
For my voice, and the other pricked out on his track.

Robert Browning,
'How They Brought the Good News from Ghent to Aix'

❦ 42 ❦

England is the paradise of women,
the purgatory of men and the hell of horses.

John Florio, *Second Frutes*

Nobody ever committed suicide
who had a good two-year-old in the barn.

Racetrack proverb

People on horses look better than they are;
people in cars look worse.

Marya Mannes

It doesn't matter what you do in the bedroom as long
as you don't do it in the street and frighten the horses.

Mrs Patrick Campbell

Before the gods that made the gods
Had seen their sunrise pass,
The White Horse of the White Horse Vale,
Was cut out of the grass.

C. K. Chesterton, 'Ballad of the White Horse'

I don't even like old cars. I mean they don't even
interest me. I'd rather have a goddam horse.
A horse is at least human for God's sake.

J. D. Salinger, *The Catcher in the Rye*

Pat: He was an Anglo-Irishman.
Meg: In the blessed name of God what's that?
Pat: A Protestant with a horse.

Brendan Behan, *The Hostage*

O happy horse, to bear the weight of Antony...

William Shakespeare, *Antony and Cleopatra*

One of the worst things that can happen in life is to
win a bet on a horse at an early age.

Danny McCoorty

Think, when we talk of horses, that you see them
Printing their proud hoofs i' th' receiving earth...

William Shakespeare, *Henry V*

'Now!' he would silently command the snorting steed.
'Now, take me to where there is luck! Now take me!'
And he would slash the horse on the neck with the
little whip he had asked Uncle Oscar for.
He knew the horse could take him to where
there was luck, if only he forced it.

D. H. Lawrence, *The Rocking-Horse Winner*

Come, let me taste my horse,
Who is to bear me like a thunderbolt...

William Shakespeare, *Henry IV*

Whilst I was young I lived upon my mother's milk, as I
could not eat grass. In the day-time I ran by her side,
and at night I lay down close by her. When it was hot,
we used to stand by the pond in the shade of the trees,
and when it was cold, we had a nice warm shed
near the plantation.

Anna Sewell, *Black Beauty*

Nester mounted the gelding by the short stirrup,
unwound his long whip, straightened his coat out from
under his knee, seated himself in the manner peculiar
to coachmen, huntsmen and horsemen,
and jerked the reins.

Leo Tolstoy, *The Story of a Horse*

It was nearly noon when Shasta was wakened by
something warm and soft moving over his face.
He opened his eyes and found himself staring into the
long face of a horse; its nose and lips
were almost touching his.

C. S. Lewis, *The Horse and His Boy*

Up and down,
          up and down,
See the plow and horses go,
Turning up the furrows brown,
     Gee wo! Gee wo!

Dicky singing loud
          and clear,
Leads his horses to and fro,
In the spring-time of the year
     Gee wo! Gee wo!

Where the brown earth
               broken lies
See the black and greedy crow
"Caw" he cries – and Dicky cries
     Gee wo! Gee wo!

Nobody has ever bet enough
on the winning horse.

Anonymous

❧ 50 ❧

Yankee Doodle went to town,
Riding on a pony;
He stuck a feather in his cap
And called it macaroni.

American nursery rhyme

I will not change my horse with any that treads...
When I bestride him, I soar, I am a hawk.
He trots the air; the earth sings when he touches it.
The basest horn of his hoof is more musical than the
pipe of Hermes...

William Shakespeare, *King Henry V*

And the Fly-Away Horse seeks those far-away lands
You little folk dream of at night –
Where candy-trees grow, and honey-brooks flow
And corn-fields with popcorn are white...

Eugene Field, 'The Fly-away Horse'

I find the Englishman to be him of all men
who stands firmest in his shoes.
They have in themselves what they value in
their horses, mettle and bottom.

Ralph Waldo Emerson

Here goes my lord
A trot, a trot, a trot, a trot!

Here goes my lady
A canter, a canter, a canter!

Here goes my young master
Jockety-hitch, jockety-hitch, jockety-hitch, jockety-hitch!

Here goes my young miss
An amble, an amble, an amble, an amble!

The footman lags behind to tipple ale and wine,
And goes gallop, a gallop, a gallop,
to make up his time.

Anonymous

Nature has not placed us in an inferior rank to men,
no more than the females of other animals,
where we see no distinction of capacity,
though I am persuaded if there was a
commonwealth of rational horses...
it would be an established maxim amongst them
that a mare could not be taught to pace.

Lady Mary Wortley Montagu

It's there you'd see the jockeys
and they mounted on most stately,
The pink and blue, the red and green,
the emblem of our nation.
When the bell was rung for starting,
the horses seemed impatient,
Though they never stood on ground,
their speed was so amazing.

Anonymous, *The Galway Races*

I had a little pony,
His name was Dapple Gray;
I lent him to a lady
To ride a mile away.
She whipped him, she slashed him,
She rode him through the mire;
I would not lend my pony now,
For all the lady's hire.

English nursery rhyme

Shoe a little horse,
Shoe a little mare,
But let the little colt
Go bare, bare, bare.

English nursery rhyme

Set a beggar on horseback,
and he'll ride to the Devil.

Proverb

NOTES ON ILLUSTRATIONS

Pages 6-7 *Ploughing* by Charles Emile Jacque (Christie's, London). Courtesy of The Bridgeman Art Library; **Pages 10-11** *Mares and Foals* by George Stubbs (Tate Gallery, London). Courtesy of The Bridgeman Art Library; **Pages 12-13** *English Horse Fair on Southborough Common* by John F. Herring Senior (Christie's, London). Courtesy of The Bridgeman Art Library; **Page 14** *Racing Horses (Before the Start)* by Edgar Degas (Musée d'Orsay, Paris). Courtesy of The Bridgeman Art Library; **Page 17** *Horse*. Courtesy of The Laurel Clark Collection; **Page 19** *Riders in the Bois de Boulogne* by Pierre Auguste Renoir (Kunsthalle, Hamburg). Courtesy of The Bridgeman Art Library; **Page 20** *The Barge Horses* by Jules Veyrassat (Christie's, London). Courtesy of The Bridgeman Art Library; **Page 22** *Outside the Stable* by Walter Hunt (Haynes Fine Art at the Bindery Galleries, Broadway). Courtesy of The Bridgeman Art Library; **Pages 24-5** *The Team* by John F. Herring Senior (Christie's, London). Courtesy of The Bridgeman Art Library; **Page 26** *Horses at Skirling Fair* by James Howe (Private Collection). Courtesy of The Bridgeman Art Library; **Page 28** *Poppy Jeannette* by Gilbert Holiday (William Marler Gallery, Cirencester). Courtesy of The Bridgeman Art Library; **Pages 32-3** *The Farmyard* by J. F. Herring Junior (Christie's, London). Courtesy of The Bridgeman Art Library; **Page 34** *Boy Leading Little Girl on Pony*. Courtesy of The Laurel Clark Collection; **Page 37** *A Carthorse Eating Hay from a Wheel-Barrow in a Farmyard* by John Frederick Herring Senior (Christie's, London). Courtesy of The Bridgeman Art Library; **Page 38** *At The Farm* by Gerhard Munthe (Nasjonalgalleriet, Oslo). Courtesy of The Bridgeman Art Library; **Page 40** *At the Water Trough in Winter* by John Frederick Herring Senior (Phillips, The International Fine Art Auctioneers). Courtesy of The Bridgeman Art Library; **Page 42** *A Wee Brown Colt*. Courtesy of The Laurel Clark Collection; **Pages 44-5** *Ploughing* by John Frederick Herring Junior (Christie's, London). Courtesy of The Bridgeman Art Library; **Page 47** *Friends* by George Armfield (Phillips, The International Fine Art Auctioneers). Courtesy of The Bridgeman Art Library; **Page 48** *Haytime Between the Showers* by Robert Thorne-Waite (Haworth Art Gallery, Accrington, Lancashire). Courtesy of The Bridgeman Art Library; **Page 50** *Up and Down, Up and Down*. Courtesy of The Laurel Clark Collection; **Pages 52-3** *The Plough Team – 1919* by Joseph Denovan Adam (Ackerman and Johnson Ltd., London). Courtesy of The Bridgeman Art Library; **Page 54** *Puss and Dobbin*. Courtesy of The Laurel Clark Collection; **Page 57** *Boy Leading Plough Horses*. Courtesy of the Laurel Clark Collection; **Pages 58-9** *Duty* by Heywood Hardy (Guildhall Art Gallery, Corporation of London). Courtesy of The Bridgeman Art Library.

Acknowledgements: The Publishers wish to thank everyone who gave permission to reproduce the quotes in this book. Every effort has been made to contact the copyright holders, but in the event that an oversight has occurred, the publishers would be delighted to rectify any omissions in future editions of this book. *Good News Study Bible*, published by Thomas Nelson, 1986, extracts reprinted with their kind permission; *Penguin Book of Japanese Verse*, translated by Geoffrey Bownas and Anthony Thwaite, published by Penguin 1964, and reprinted with their permission; Beatrix Potter reproduced courtesy of Frederick Warne & Co., a division of Penguin Books; Carmen Bernos de Casztold, from 'The Prayer of the Foal' from *Prayers from the Ark*, translated by Rumer Godden, reprinted courtesy of Macmillan Publishing Company Ltd; D. H. Lawrence, from *The Complete Poems of D. H. Lawrence*, edited by Vivian de Sola Pinto and F. Warren Roberts, copyright © 1964, 1971 by Angelo Ravagli and C. M. Weekley, Executors of the Estate of Frieda Lawrence Ravagli. Used by permission of Laurence Pollinger Ltd and Viking Penguin, a division of Penguin Books USA Inc.; G. K. Chesterton reprinted courtesy of Methuen and Dodd Mead, copyright renewed; Rudyard Kipling, reprinted courtesy of Macmillan Publishing Company Limited; John Masefield, reprinted courtesy of Reed Books and the Literary Trustees of John Masefield and The Society of Authors as their representative; J. D. Salinger reprinted courtesy of Penguin Books; Jilly Cooper, from *Polo*, published by Bantam Press and reprinted with their permission © Jilly Cooper, 1991; Monica Dickens, *Mariana*, first published by Michael Joseph, reprinted courtesy of Penguin Books © Monica Dickens, 1940; Hilaire Belloc, reprinted from *The Complete Verse of Hilaire Belloc*, by permission of Peters Fraser and Dunlop Group Ltd; *The Horse and His Boy*, C. S. Lewis © C. S. Lewis, 1950, reprinted by permission of HarperCollins Publishers Ltd.